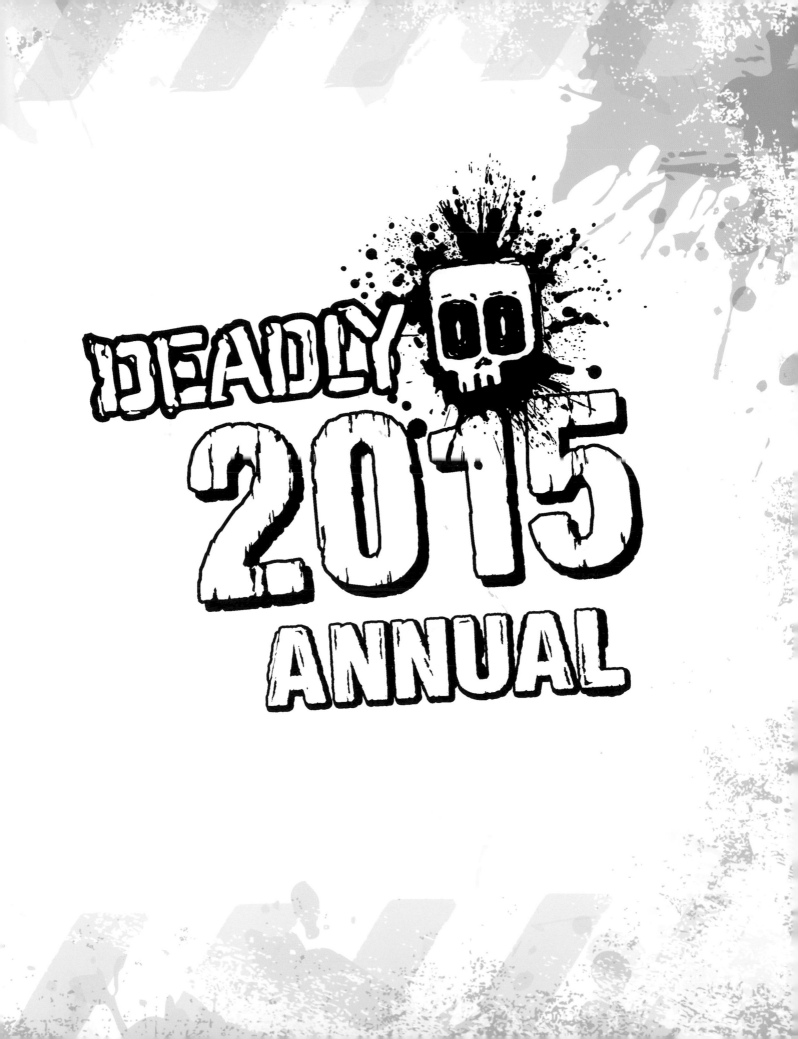

DEADLY 2015 ANNUAL

Orion
Children's Books

WELCOME

TO THE 2015 DEADLY ANNUAL!

As a Deadly fan you know that we travel to all corners of the world to film and this time we're on our deadliest mission yet! We visit the driest deserts, the steamiest rainforests, the highest mountains and the snowiest forests in search of the most awesome wildlife. As ever, you're coming with us, every step of the way.

Join us on a journey round the world and we'll tell you more about these incredible places and the animals that spend their lives there. We've got loads of fascinating facts to share with you, as well as plenty of puzzles, pictures and fun stuff to enjoy!

PORTRAIT OF A PREDATOR: KILLER WHALE

You can spot a killer whale by the tall fin on its back, which rises high above the ocean surface. This magnificent black and white whale, also known as the orca, is found in all the world's oceans, including the Arctic and the Southern Ocean around the Antarctic.

Killer whales are among the most intelligent and efficient of all hunters. They prey on other marine mammals such as seals and sea lions as well as on fish and birds. Few creatures are a match for these mighty predators and they will even tackle other kinds of whale.

Killer whales have many clever ways of catching their prey. In the Antarctic, they have been seen creating waves to knock seals or penguins off ice floes. They also hunt by driving other whales under the surface to drown them.

They usually live in groups, called pods. The orcas in a pod communicate with each other using a range of sounds and often work as a team to overcome their prey. They are fast swimmers and can speed through the water at 40 kilometres an hour.

Male killer whales can measure 9.8 metres, weigh as much as 9,000 kilograms – more than 5 average cars – and have sleek streamlined bodies. Females are smaller than males, weighing about 5,500 kilograms.

Sharp teeth, about 10 centimetres long

Paddle-shaped pectoral fins

Back fin, up to 1.8 metres long in males

Broad head

The **WOLVERINE** is a member of the weasel family. It is a fearsome, strong-jawed creature that will eat any carrion (animals that are already dead) it comes across and also attacks prey bigger than itself. Its jaws are so powerful it can even crunch through frozen meat so can feast on the carcasses of animals that might have died of cold in the forest.

The wolverine is only about a metre long but hugely powerful. A wolverine has been known to bring down caribou – a kind of large deer that can be 15 times the predator's weight.

The **BLACK BEAR** lives in northern North America, usually in forests, and is a good tree climber. It has a varied diet, eating roots, berries, insects and grass as well as fish and other animals. Human food waste is very appealing to these bears and they often overturn rubbish bins to get food.

A full-grown black bear can be up to about 1.8 metres long and weigh 270 kilograms, although most are smaller. A sturdy animal with big teeth and claws, it can be dangerous if it feels threatened.

Winters are hard in the forest and the bear may spend as long as 6 months asleep in a den in a cave or burrow or even in hollow trees. It does not eat during this time but may wake up from time to time. The female gives birth to cubs in mid-winter. She can have up to 5 but 2–3 is more usual. The family stays in the den until spring and warmer weather, when the cubs emerge for the first time.

The **GREAT GREY OWL** is the biggest – but not the heaviest – owl in North America and it lives in the far northern forests.

To hunt, the owl perches in the trees, listening for the slightest sound of small mammals such as mice and voles below. It has incredible hearing and can hear its prey moving, even under thick snow. The owl then swoops down and seizes the prey in its needle-sharp talons.

The **GREAT GREY SHRIKE**, also known as the northern shrike, catches other birds, insects and small mammals. It hunts from a perch but also attacks prey in trees and snatches insects in the air.

Another name for this shrike is the butcherbird because of its habit of impaling prey on thorns and barbed wire. This holds the meal firmly in place while the shrike pulls it apart with its hooked beak.

This tough little bird is about 25 centimetres long.

The **POLECAT** is a wily hunter with a long slender body and short legs. It is usually active at night and will attack any prey it can find, such as rats, frogs, birds and insects.

It can produce a very smelly substance from glands near its tail, which sends the message, 'Keep away from me'. It uses this to warn off enemies.

There are several species of polecat. The European polecat lives in northern forests as well as areas farther south.

The howl of a **GREY WOLF** is one of the familiar sounds of the northern forest. Wolves hunt in packs of about 5–9 animals – sometimes many more – and work together to bring down prey such deer. They also catch and eat smaller mammals as well as birds and lizards. A dominant male and female lead the pack, which is usually made up of their young of various years.

Wolves travel long distances in search of prey and can run at speeds of up to 70 kilometres an hour. They are the largest wild dogs and can weigh 70 kilograms, although most are smaller.

NORTHERN FOREST ANIMAL WORDSEARCH

All these animals live in northern forests.
Can you find their names in this wordsearch puzzle?

R	C	T	O	E	T	I	E	W	M	S	A	S	E	S
E	E	G	N	F	B	I	H	T	O	E	R	F	U	R
N	R	D	P	H	E	A	S	A	N	T	H	N	A	F
I	A	E	S	G	I	E	R	T	F	E	U	O	D	N
R	S	I	I	Q	R	A	E	B	K	C	A	L	B	H
E	P	L	B	N	U	O	N	W	A	T	G	I	E	R
V	O	A	A	G	D	I	O	T	E	U	O	F	D	E
L	L	R	T	E	N	E	R	E	H	E	S	D	O	K
O	E	S	I	T	E	I	E	R	E	M	H	O	T	C
W	C	F	A	S	I	E	M	R	E	L	A	T	E	E
E	A	G	L	E	O	W	L	M	D	L	W	S	R	P
B	T	E	S	M	L	H	K	I	E	I	K	N	S	D
E	I	Y	F	J	A	Y	P	I	O	L	E	S	A	O
R	E	D	D	E	E	R	N	H	S	O	H	R	O	O
U	S	A	E	E	U	E	E	X	I	A	N	T	D	W

BLACK BEAR
LEMMING
WOLVERINE

WOODPECKER
RED SQUIRREL
EAGLE OWL

LYNX
RED DEER
POLECAT

REINDEER
GOSHAWK
PHEASANT

PORTRAIT OF A PREDATOR: LYNX

The lynx has an amazing ability to spring up from the ground to catch low-flying birds. It is also a skilful climber, its claws acting like crampons to help it cling to tree trunks with great ease.

This cat's spotted coat becomes particularly long and thick in winter to keep it warm through the snowy months. Even its paws are covered in fur to help it move on icy ground. On its ears are little tufts of black fur, which seem to make the lynx's already acute hearing even better.

The lynx is one of the largest predators in northern forests. It generally hunts at night by stealth, hiding in the forest undergrowth and creeping up on prey until it is as close as possible. It then makes a final deadly pounce to seize its kill. Lynx can overcome animals several times their own size, such as deer, but smaller creatures such as beavers, rabbits, mice and birds are also caught.

The Eurasian lynx lives in northern Europe and Asia, and the Canada lynx in northern North America. At about 1.3 metres long, the Eurasian lynx is slightly bigger than the Canadian species.

Tufty ears

Shaggy coat

Sharp teeth

Long legs – the back
legs are longer than
front legs to help the
lynx pounce

Chunky paws

Wolverine

Skill Level: Medium

The wolverine is one of the fiercest hunters in the northern forests and can climb trees and swim across rivers as it searches for prey.

1. Start with 2 upside-down L shapes in the middle of the page. Draw a big hill for the head on top and add 2 oval shapes for the ears. Add a big C shape at the side.

2. Add 2 ovals for the paws and draw 4 lines in each for the claws. Now take your marker pen and go over the head and ears and add some lines to the inside of the ears. Draw triangles for the eyes.

3. Go over the L shapes in marker and add some zigzag shapes for the fur. Add in the nose and 2 upside-down triangles for the deadly teeth. Draw a line out from between the teeth to make the gaping mouth.

4. Go round the C shape with zigzag lines for fur. Then draw in those deadly claws with marker pen, adding knuckles on top of the claws.

5. Finally, add more jagged teeth to that snarling mouth, making them smaller towards the centre. There's your deadly wolverine.

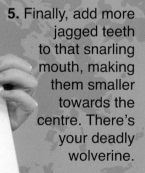

Jo from the Deadly Art team

CHAPTER 3
DESERTS

DID YOU KNOW?

 Not all deserts are endless stretches of sand and sand dunes. Some have rocky, pebbly ground with a few scrubby plants, while others are mountainous. Deserts may look empty but in fact there are many animals and plants that have adapted to life in these difficult conditions.

There are hot deserts and cold deserts. The Sahara in North Africa is the world's largest hot desert. It is about 9,000,000 square kilometres. Temperatures there can reach a scorching 50°C in the daytime but it is much colder at night. To give you an idea of just how hot that is, the highest temperature ever recorded in Britain was 38.5°C, in August 2003.

 A desert is a place where less than 25 centimetres of rain falls in a year. Deserts cover about 20 per cent of our planet.

DESERT ANIMAL FACTS

The **OSTRICH** is the world's largest bird. It can't fly but does run extremely fast, at up to 70 kilometres an hour. The fastest human runners move at 44.7 kilometres an hour and only for short distances. Ostriches live in desert and dry grassland and rarely drink water. The plants they eat provide most of the water they need but they also catch insects and lizards.

One of the largest lizards in North America, the **GILA MONSTER** lives in desert areas and grows to up to 58 centimetres long. This creature has a venomous bite, which it generally uses to defend itself.

This lizard avoids the desert heat by spending much of its time hiding in underground burrows. Food can be scarce, but when the gila monster does find prey or birds' eggs it can eat as much as 35 per cent of its own weight. One good meal keeps it going for weeks. It also stores fat in its tail for when times are hard.

An ostrich can be 2.7 metres tall and weighs 160 kilograms. It has the largest eyes of any land animal. They measure as much as 5 centimetres across – that's almost the size of a tennis ball. To defend itself, the ostrich can lash out with its feet. Each foot bears a 10-centimetre long claw, which can deliver a nasty wound.

People used to think that the ostrich buried its head in the sand in an attempt to hide from enemies but this isn't true. What the ostrich does do is press its neck down on the ground if danger threatens to try and make itself less obvious.

The **FENNEC FOX** lives in the Sahara desert in Africa and can survive with very little water. It gets what it needs from its food and prevents water loss by sheltering from the daytime heat in an underground burrow. Its super-sized ears help it lose heat and stay cool – and they also pick up the slightest sound of prey scurrying in the sand. This fox's feet are covered with hair to protect it as it walks on burning hot sand.

Fennec foxes aren't fussy about food and eat almost anything they can find, including insects, eggs, rats and mice and plants.

PORTRAIT OF A PREDATOR: WESTERN DIAMONDBACK RATTLESNAKE

An expert desert hunter, the rattlesnake lies in wait for prey, flicking its forked tongue in and out to pick up any scent particles. When a victim comes close enough, the snake makes a rapid strike with its needle-sharp fangs. These inject deadly venom into the prey, which soon dies. The snake cannot chew so swallows its meal whole – the venom also helps break down the prey once it is inside the snake.

The rattlesnake uses sight and smell to detect its quarry but it also hunts by sensing the heat given off by warm-blooded animals. Heat-detecting organs on its head that look like little pits enable the snake to 'see' the prey's body heat in the dark and so catch it with ease.

The rattlesnake's rattle is used to warn off enemies. The sound it makes sends the message, 'Stay away or there could be trouble!' A young snake starts with just a button-shaped tip to its tail. Each time it sheds its skin a segment is left behind and these make up the rattle. When the snake shakes its tail the rattle makes the buzzing noise that gives the snake its name.

Pit organ between nostril and eye

Up to 1.5 metres long and weighs 6.7 kilograms

Rattle at the end of the tail

PORTRAIT OF A PREDATOR: GOLIATH BIRD-EATING SPIDER

The world's largest tarantula and one of the biggest and heaviest of all spiders, the goliath bird-eating spider is a formidable sight. Its body is nearly 12 centimetres long and its hairy legs span 28 centimetres – the width of a dinner plate. Its fangs can measure 2.5 centimetres. But despite its menacing appearance the spider is not really dangerous to humans, although its bite is painful.

This spider lives in the Amazon rainforest where it shelters in a burrow that it lines with silk. It is certainly big and strong enough to catch birds but more often feeds on rats, mice, lizards and insects. It usually hunts at night and knows when prey is near by sensing the vibrations on the ground. It then pounces out of its burrow and bites the victim with its fangs, injecting venom.

If the spider is threatened, it first hisses at its attacker by rubbing its front legs together. If this doesn't scare off the enemy it starts to flick little hairs off its body. These cause irritation and itching to the attacker, particularly if they land in the eyes or mouth.

Female bird-eaters live for 20 years or more – much longer than males. Some males are eaten or injured by females after mating.

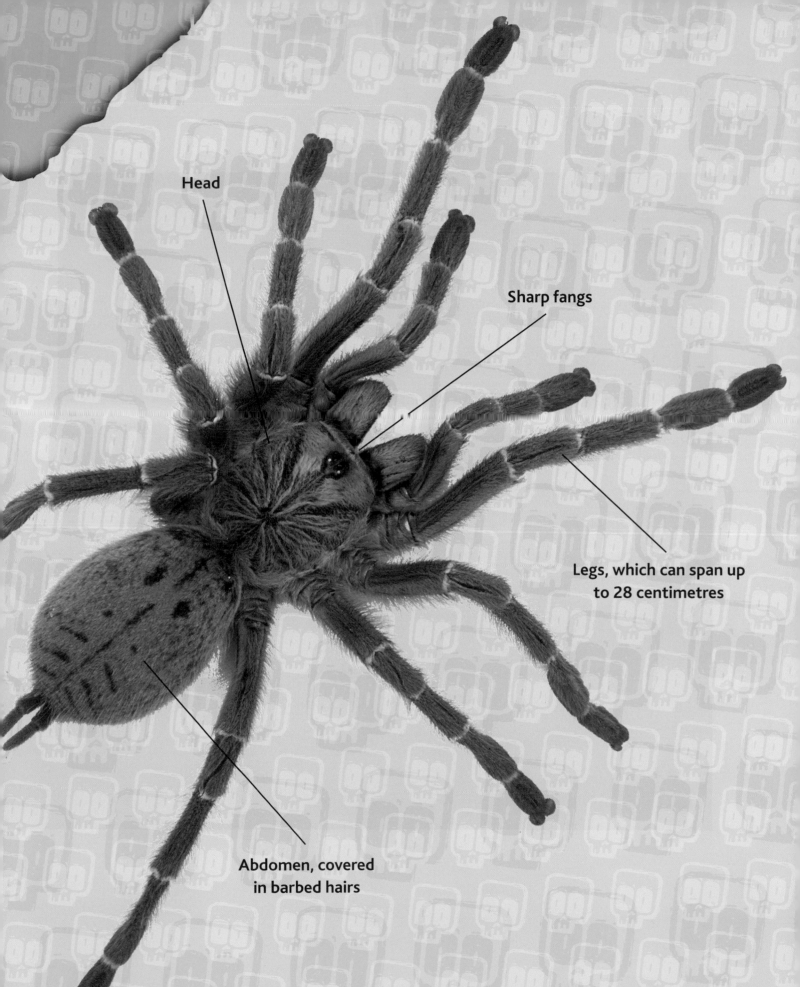

Head

Sharp fangs

Legs, which can span up
to 28 centimetres

Abdomen, covered
in barbed hairs

CHAPTER 5
GRASSLAND

DID YOU KNOW?

Vast, open plains like seas of grass cover as much as a quarter of all our planet's land and there are grasslands on every continent except Antarctica. They are known by different names, such as steppe, prairie and savanna, depending on where they are.

Grasslands grow where there is too much rain for desert to form but not enough for forest. There are usually few trees.

Some grasslands are in tropical areas where it is warm all year round but there are dry and rainy seasons. Others are in cooler temperate regions where summers are hot and winters cold.

Lots of plant-eating animals live on grasslands and feed on the grasses and other plants. And where there are plant-eaters there are predators to feed on them.

GRASSLAND ANIMAL FACTS

One of the fastest-running animals in North America, the **PRONGHORN** can sprint at 86 kilometres an hour for brief periods to escape from its predators. It can also run at about 70 kilometres an hour for longer distances.

Pronghorns live on grassland, known as prairie, in North America and feed on grass. They look like antelope although they actually have their own special scientific family. Both male and female pronghorn have horns that can be a much as 30 centimetres long.

SPOTTED HYENAS patrol the savanna, Africa's grassland, preying on animals such as antelope and zebra. They often hunt in groups to bring down animals much larger than themselves. Hyenas are also well known for scavenging and they will feed on dead animals and the leftovers of other predators' kills. Their jaws and teeth are so strong that they can even crunch through bones.

KANGAROOS live on grasslands and other habitats in Australia. With their long back legs, they can cover great distances as they travel in search of fresh grass to eat. A kangaroo can hop along at 64 kilometres an hour and cover 9 metres in a single bound.

The red kangaroo (right) is up to 1.6 metres long with a metre-long tail and can weigh 90 kilograms. The grey kangaroo (below) is slightly smaller. Although kangaroos are plant eaters, not predators, their size and strength make them dangerous. They have vicious claws on their feet and can deliver a nasty kick with those strong back legs.

PORTRAIT OF A PREDATOR: AFRICAN HUNTING DOG

DEADLY

African hunting dogs are pack hunters. They live in close-knit groups of 10 or more animals, which work together to chase and bring down antelopes and other large plant eaters. A male and female pair usually leads the pack. They are the only members of the pack that breed and they have young, which the rest of the pack helps to look after.

Mottled markings on coat – each animal has a slightly different pattern

Big, rounded ears

Long legs

The dogs can use their keen eyes to spot prey on the grassy plains. They are fast runners and can move at speeds of as much as 65 kilometres an hour as they close in for the kill. As they reach the victim, the dogs snap at its tail and hindquarters, grabbing anything they can to weaken the animal and drag it to the ground. These dogs have powerful jaw muscles that help them hang on to prey. The whole pack shares in the kill, even old or injured dogs that haven't taken part in the hunt, and pups are allowed to take the first bites.

African hunting dogs will tackle anything from wildebeest to rats and birds.

Vulture

Skill Level: Hard

Like all vultures, the white-backed vulture feeds mostly on carrion – animals that are already dead. It has long broad wings that help it soar for hours as it searches for food and it also has excellent eyesight. Its head is bare of feathers so that it doesn't get too messy when feeding.

1. Start by drawing a simple rugby ball shape. Then add 2 circles and next to them, a long triangle. At the bottom, draw 2 sets of 4 short lines – these will be the feet.

2. Take a black marker pen and draw in the sharp hooked beak on top of the rugby ball shape. Add the vulture's beady eye.

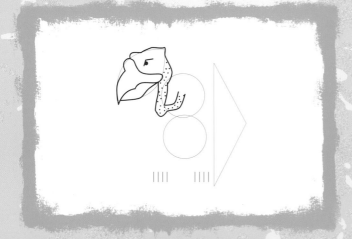

3. Link the head to the top circle with a scraggy bent neck. Add some dots for stubby feathers.

4. With the marker pen, draw some thick zigzag lines round the body outlines to look like feathers.

5. For the big wings, draw some big arches over your triangle guidelines and add zigzag edges. Draw in the deadly claws with marker pen.

6. Now give your vulture something to sit on. Draw in a long branch extending at each side of the feet and between the feet.

CHAPTER 6
MOUNTAINS

DID YOU KNOW?

There are towering mountain ranges on every continent of the world. Mountains cover about a fifth of our planet and there are even some massive peaks under the sea.

The higher up a mountain you go the colder it is and the fewer trees there are so mountain tops are often bare of plants. Life is hard for animals on mountains but some have found ways to survive.

The world's highest mountain above sea level is Mount Everest in the Himalayas in Asia. It measures about 8,848 metres high.

There is a volcano in Hawaii called Mauna Kea, which starts deep in the Pacific Ocean. If this mountain is measured from its base, under the sea, it is an awesome 10,210 metres but only 4,205 metres of this are above sea level.

MOUNTAIN ANIMAL FACTS

GIANT PANDAS live in bamboo forests in the mountains of central China. Although a panda does sometimes eat small animals, bamboo is its main food. The plant it is not very nourishing for an animal of this size so the panda has to spend most of its day eating.

A panda's teeth are wide and flat for grinding up the tough bamboo and it also has an extra 'thumb', made from the wrist bone, on each front paw that helps it hold the stalks while it eats.

The **LAMMERGEIER**'s huge wings measure up to 3 metres from tip to tip. They allow this awesome vulture to soar over mountains with hardly a wingbeat as it searches for food.

The bones of carrion are its favourite food. It can eat small bones whole but it has a clever trick with larger bones. It carries them up into the air and then drops them on to rocks where they break into pieces. The lammergeier then flies down again and feeds on the nourishing marrow inside the bones. It also hunts live prey such as tortoises and hares.

The **SNOW LEOPARD** lives in mountainous parts of the Gobi Desert as well as in other parts of Central Asia. It can be very cold there but the snow leopard is kept warm by its very dense soft fur, which becomes extra thick during the winter. Its large paws act like snowshoes to help it walk on snow.

The snow leopard's speckled, greyish coat helps to keep it hidden in its rocky home as it creeps up on prey such as wild sheep and goats. It leaps from crag to crag with ease, using its long furry tail to help it balance.

Tragically poachers kill snow leopards for their beautiful fur and they are also shot for their body parts, used in traditional Asian medicine. Farmers sometimes hunt snow leopards that prey on their livestock. The snow leopard is now an endangered species and there may be only 4,000-6,000 left in the wild.

The **ANDEAN CONDOR** is one of the largest and heaviest of all flying birds. This scavenger lives in South America where it glides over the Andes mountains on its long wings, searching for dead animals to eat. The mountain winds and air currents help this enormous bird stay aloft.

The **MOUNTAIN LION**, also called the puma or cougar, is a superb predator, which hunts animals such as deer, porcupines and raccoons. It generally searches for food at night and has far better night vision than we do. A stealthy killer, it sneaks as close as it can get to prey, then makes a lethal pounce and kills it with a bite to the back of the neck. It makes remarkable jumps and can leap up into trees when chasing a meal.

Mountain lions live in North and South America in habitats from desert to jungle as well as mountains. They can make a variety of calls, such as growls and whistles, but cannot roar.

MOUNTAIN ANIMAL WORDSEARCH

All these animals live in mountainous areas.
Can you find their names in this wordsearch puzzle?

L	R	M	O	U	N	T	A	I	N	L	I	O	N	M
A	O	E	R	E	T	R	A	N	S	T	E	T	O	O
M	D	T	L	R	A	O	D	I	A	A	O	U	O	S
M	N	R	A	E	B	N	W	O	R	B	N	E	C	T
E	O	P	E	E	H	S	N	I	A	T	N	U	O	M
R	C	E	T	A	W	S	T	Y	A	A	I	T	E	U
G	N	I	E	N	M	E	I	I	F	O	O	B	T	M
E	A	E	L	G	A	E	N	E	D	L	O	G	E	P
I	E	V	E	R	C	G	U	A	N	A	C	O	I	X
E	D	O	F	H	O	A	A	R	E	I	E	H	S	H
R	N	T	U	R	K	E	Y	V	U	L	T	U	R	E
B	A	G	I	A	N	T	P	A	N	D	A	N	N	I
O	N	L	V	L	X	E	S	C	H	M	E	R	G	R
Y	L	H	E	I	R	E	T	T	M	T	P	E	Y	S
A	D	R	A	P	O	E	L	W	O	N	S	E	O	E

LAMMERGEIER   **MOUNTAIN GORILLA**   **IBEX**   **GOLDEN EAGLE**

GIANT PANDA   **ANDEAN CONDOR**   **GUANACO**   **MOUNTAIN LION**

SNOW LEOPARD   **MOUNTAIN SHEEP**   **BROWN BEAR**   **TURKEY VULTURE**

PORTRAIT OF A PREDATOR: GOLDEN EAGLE

An impressive bird of prey, the golden eagle lives in mountain areas in North America, Africa, Europe and Asia.

This sharp-eyed bird is an expert predator. It soars high over the ground searching for prey and can spot a likely meal from 2 kilometres away. When it has located its victim, the eagle plunges down at speeds of 225 kilometres an hour to seize and kill prey with its dagger-like talons. It then tears its meal apart with its strong beak.

Mammals such as rabbits and ground squirrels are the golden eagle's main food, but it is strong enough to kill larger animals such as sheep and eats carrion.

Golden eagle pairs mate for life and build an enormous nest, known as an eyrie, in a tree or on a cliff ledge where they lay their eggs. They may use this nest year after year, adding to it each time. Some eagle nests can be a metre or more across and as much as 3 metres high – roomy enough for a person to hide in!

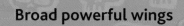

Broad powerful wings

Long tail

Large eyes

Hooked beak

Talons up to 5 centimetres long

63

CHAPTER 7
OCEANS

DID YOU KNOW?

There are 5 oceans: Pacific, Atlantic, Indian, Arctic and Southern.

The deepest point of all the oceans is in the Pacific. It is called the Mariana Trench and it is about 11,034 metres deep.

The Pacific Ocean is the largest and is about twice the size of the Atlantic Ocean. The Pacific covers about 165.25 million square kilometres – about 30 per cent of the Earth's surface.

About 71 per cent of our planet is covered by oceans.

of any mammal. There are as many as 100,000 hairs in every square centimetre.

Hard-shelled sea creatures such as mussels, clams and sea urchins are the main food of the sea otter. It often uses a rock to crack open its meals and it is one of the few animals to use tools in this way.

A deadly monster of the deep sea, the **HUMBOLDT SQUID** can be 2 metres long. Its long tentacles are lined with barbed suckers and used to capture prey such as fish, shellfish and even other squid. The squid tears its meal apart with its sharp beak, which looks rather like a parrot's beak but is made of different material and is much harder and incredibly tough.

This squid can swim at 24 kilometres an hour. If attacked, it can squirt ink from special sacs in its body at its enemy.

A ferocious predator on coral reefs is the **CROWN-OF-THORNS STARFISH**. This creature can be as much as 1 metre across and has as many as 21 arms, all covered with venomous spines. It crawls over the coral reef, killing and eating the defenceless coral animals.

The crown-of-thorn's feeding method is simple. It throws the lining of its stomach out through its mouth over the coral and special juices in its stomach kill and digest the coral. The starfish then pulls its stomach – and its meal – back into its body and moves on.

OCEAN ANIMAL WORDSEARCH

All these animals live in the oceans.
Can you find their names in this wordsearch puzzle?

B	E	A	O	S	A	A	O	A	K	V	S	D	E	H
I	O	D	D	N	C	C	I	R	E	P	I	I	L	S
Y	E	X	U	U	T	T	A	F	E	T	N	U	A	I
V	A	L	J	O	C	H	T	R	H	O	D	Q	H	F
R	S	R	P	E	S	A	M	T	A	F	S	S	W	D
T	E	U	G	R	L	W	R	I	E	D	A	T	E	R
N	S	T	E	N	H	L	L	R	O	T	C	N	U	O
V	E	G	T	A	I	I	Y	L	A	S	U	A	L	W
P	I	I	L	O	O	T	P	F	A	B	Q	I	B	S
T	I	E	G	N	A	H	S	T	I	O	M	G	Y	R
U	E	E	F	O	I	E	S	E	O	S	F	F	E	T
G	W	I	V	N	D	R	S	F	O	A	H	I	T	A
H	S	E	A	M	O	G	Y	E	M	L	R	S	I	R
H	H	E	S	I	B	R	E	I	O	A	T	N	Y	E
M	F	Y	S	F	R	T	O	D	N	E	N	E	B	C

TIGER SHARK	**SPERM WHALE**	**OCTOPUS**	**STINGRAY**
BLUE WHALE	**SWORDFISH**	**DOLPHIN**	**BARRACUDA**
GIANT SQUID	**BOX JELLYFISH**	**LIONFISH**	**SEA OTTER**

PORTRAIT OF A PREDATOR: GREAT WHITE SHARK

The great white is a top predator in the world's oceans. This spectacular hunter can be 6.4 metres long – longer than an average family car – and can weigh as much as 3,400 kilograms. Females are usually bigger than males.

The great white's streamlined body cruises through the water at about 40 kilometres an hour but it can speed up to 56 kilometres an hour for short bursts. Its skin is covered with scales, called denticles, which look like tiny teeth. These help the shark move fast through the water by reducing drag. In fact, this works so well that suits with a similar surface are made for Olympic swimmers!

The shark's huge jaws are lined with 7 rows of serrated teeth – up to 300 in all. These teeth are deadly sharp and can be 7.5 centimetres long. The great white does not chew its food but tears it into pieces to swallow.

Few creatures can escape the great white's toothy jaws because it also has extraordinarily acute senses. Most important of all is smell and the great white's sense of smell is so acute that it could smell a single drop of blood in 10 billion drops of water. The shark's sight and hearing are super-keen too and it can detect the slightest vibrations in water made by prey.

Great whites can tackle almost any other animal but they have a great enemy – us. Every year millions of sharks are killed by humans. Some are hunted deliberately for use in shark fin soup – considered a delicacy in some Asian countries. Others die by accident in fishing nets or are killed by pollution. These amazing creatures are becoming increasingly rare and deserve our protection.

First 2 rows of teeth are used to attack prey, with others ready to move into place if any are damaged or lost

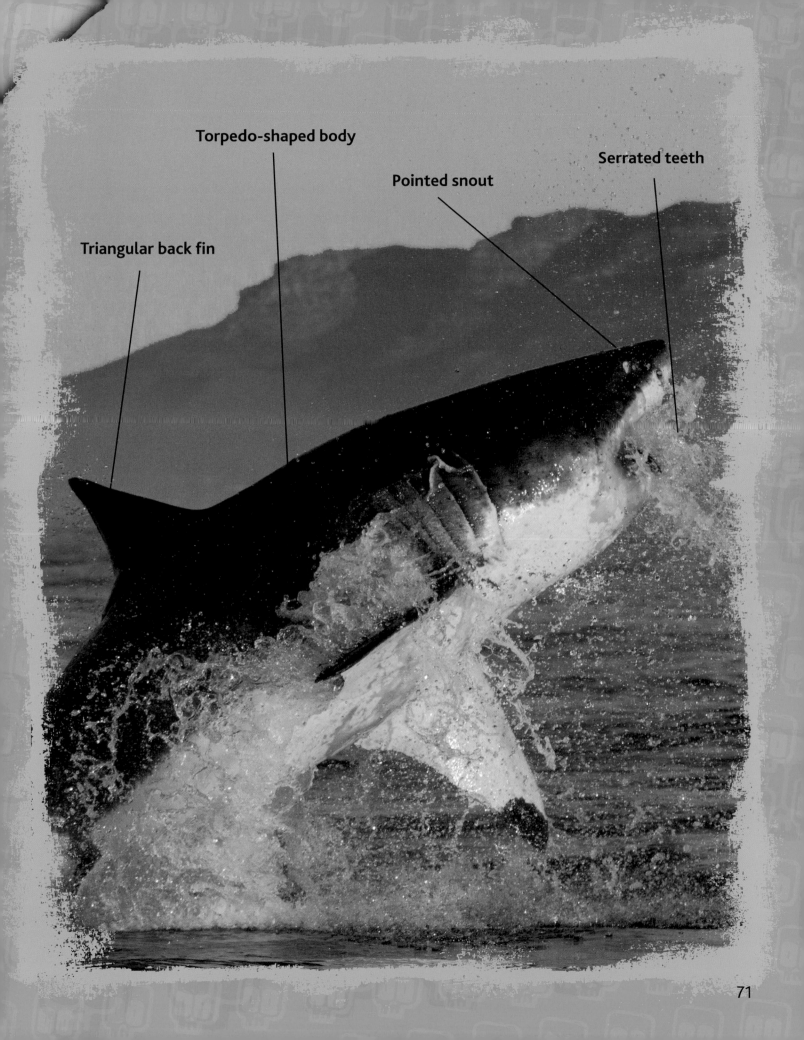

Triangular back fin

Torpedo-shaped body

Pointed snout

Serrated teeth

All the answers to the quiz are somewhere in this book.
Try it yourself and then test your friends!

1 Where does the polar bear live?
a In the Arctic
b In Antarctica

2 Where do emperor penguins live?
a In the Arctic
b In Antarctica

3 Which animal family does the wolverine belong to?
a The dog family
b The bear family
c The weasel family

4 Where is the world's biggest hot desert?
a South America
b Africa
c Asia

5 Which is the world's largest bird?
a The ostrich
b The golden eagle
c The condor

6 How many humps does a Dromedary camel have?
a One
b Two

7 Where is the world's biggest rainforest?
a South America
b Africa
c Australia

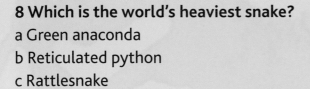

11 Where does the snow leopard live?
a South America
b Africa
c Asia

12 What is the lammergeier?
a A bird
b A fish
c A lizard

8 Which is the world's heaviest snake?
a Green anaconda
b Reticulated python
c Rattlesnake

9 Which is the world's largest ocean?
a Atlantic
b Pacific
c Indian

10 Which animal makes the loudest call?
a Blue whale
b Lion
c Elephant

73

PUZZLE ANSWERS

Here you will find all the answers to the puzzles shown in this book. Have fun . . .

p25 NORTHERN FOREST ANIMAL WORDSEARCH

R	C	T	O	E	T	I	E	W	M	S	A	S	E	S
E	E	G	N	F	B	I	H	T	O	E	R	F	U	R
N	R	D	P	H	E	A	S	A	N	T	H	N	A	F
I	A	E	S	G	I	E	R	T	F	E	U	O	D	N
R	S	I	I	Q	R	A	E	B	K	C	A	L	B	H
E	P	L	B	N	U	O	N	W	A	T	G	I	E	R
V	O	A	A	G	D	I	O	T	E	U	O	F	D	E
L	L	R	T	E	N	E	R	E	H	E	S	D	O	K
O	E	S	I	T	E	I	E	R	E	M	H	O	T	C
W	C	F	A	S	I	E	M	R	E	L	A	T	E	E
E	A	G	L	E	O	W	L	M	D	L	W	S	R	P
B	T	E	S	M	L	H	K	I	E	I	K	N	S	D
E	I	Y	F	J	A	Y	P	I	O	L	E	S	A	O
R	E	D	D	E	E	R	N	H	S	O	H	R	O	O
U	S	A	E	E	U	E	E	X	I	A	N	T	D	W

p17 POLAR ANIMAL WORDSEARCH

L	A	N	S	P	D	N	L	T	W	K	O	O	E	K
T	A	N	I	N	O	W	L	R	R	I	G	M	H	I
O	S	E	T	U	O	L	E	D	O	E	P	N	M	L
S	A	R	S	Y	G	W	A	A	T	E	N	H	T	L
E	M	D	W	R	S	N	G	R	R	O	R	T	E	E
O	T	O	R	U	E	S	E	O	B	F	D	T	N	R
X	N	S	R	V	E	T	R	P	O	E	I	M	W	W
S	O	L	R	I	A	P	A	T	G	S	A	I	F	H
R	A	K	E	R	E	O	H	E	N	N	E	R	A	A
W	A	S	S	N	T	M	N	D	B	B	I	H	S	L
N	D	T	G	U	L	A	G	E	A	A	A	K	D	E
A	C	U	H	A	M	T	A	F	E	E	R	E	I	I
E	I	A	R	C	T	I	C	F	O	X	A	C	S	R
N	L	E	O	P	A	R	D	S	E	A	L	G	S	H
P	U	F	F	I	N	N	O	D	T	E	A	D	H	E

p35 DESERT ANIMAL CRISS-CROSS

OSTRICH
SCORPION
ROADRUNNER
CAMEL
RATTLESNAKE
MEERKAT
LOCUST
AARDVARK
SIDEWINDER

p43 RAINFOREST ANIMAL WORDSEARCH

```
P N E L O N O W T D F N U W T
O A H T T V T N E Q A G N I L
I T P R N A I E E M U T I R L
S U E R E N R V I Y S C H L O
O G T A E L G A E Y P R A H C
N N L R V E C E N I I T E N E
D A A T U K T J T T E E C A L
A R L L C I A T G T U E R C O
R O N A L G T N F A R L A L T
T F L S U I S B A N N C A T D
F B A A G L R V A C O A U S O
R E R F O O D Q E T O S E T E
O I T T R O T U G A H N A T U
G A H U I D R E S O I N D E U
R G I L H T R E N G D M E A T
```

p61 MOUNTAIN ANIMAL WORDSEARCH

```
L R M O U N T A I N L I O N M
A O E R E T R A N S T E T O O
M D T L R A O D L A A O U O S
M N R A E B N W O R B N E C T
E O P E E H S N I A T N U O M
R C E T A W S T Y A A I T E U
G N I E N M E I I F O O B T M
E A E L G A E N E D L O G E P
I E V E R C G U A N A C O I X
E D O F H O A A R E I E H S H
R N T U R K E Y V U L T U R E
B A G I A N T P A N D A N N I
O N L V L X E S C H M E R G R
Y L H E I R E T T M T P E Y S
A D R A P O E L W O N S E O E
```

p51 GRASSLAND ANIMAL CRISS-CROSS

p69 OCEAN ANIMAL WORDSEARCH

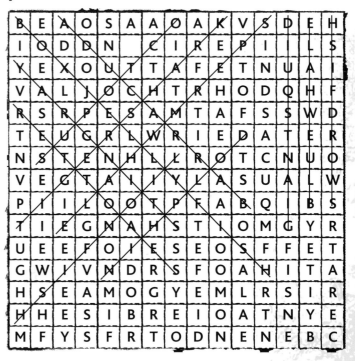

p71 DEADLY 60 QUIZ

1 a; 2 b; 3 c; 4 b; 5 a; 6 a; 7 a; 8 a; 9 b; 10 a; 11 c; 12 a

For a truly DEADLY year in 2015, collect all the DEADLY books . . .

Look out for the **brand new DEADLY** Sticker book - with **over** 200 stickers inside.

Find out **fascinating facts** in the brilliant **DEADLY** factbooks

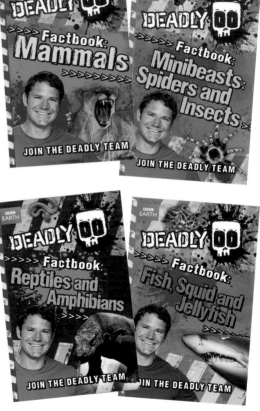

Read about Steve's adventures filming **DEADLY** in his very own **Deadly Diaries**.

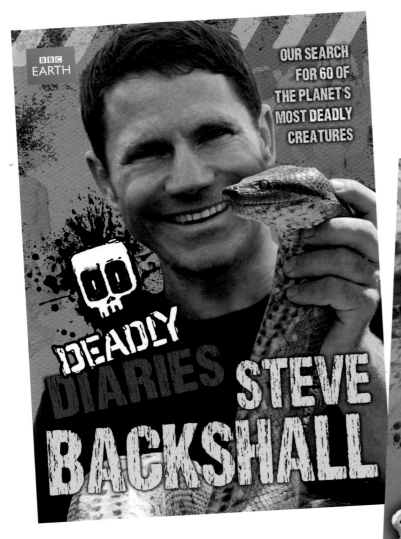

Or, stay closer to home as a **Deadly Detective**, and discover deadly creatures in your own back garden.

And don't miss Steve's **Deadliest** journey yet in **Pole To Pole Diaries**.

JOIN THE DEADLY ADVENTURE!